10 Seconds is
Changing Lives Forever

LETTERS OF HOPE

Bobby Petrocelli

Published by Bobby Petrocelli, 10 Seconds, Inc.
P.O. Box 923
Bellport, NY 11713
800-547-7933

Additional copies of this book can be obtained by visiting:

www.10Seconds.org

www.10secondscanchangeyourlifeforever.com

Printed in the United States of America
Print and Bind Direct!
books@PrintAndBind.com

Table of Contents

Section 6

Section 7

Section 8

Section 9

Section 10

Section 11

Introduction

My ultimate desire is that you will find Hope, Faith, and Love in every area of your life. The following pages contain actual letters, written by students, teachers, administrators, parents and many others who have heard me in person, in one of my live speeches. I've also included many inspirational quotes that will help you each time you read them. Together they will lift your spirit at any time of day or night. In my years of traveling and speaking full-time, I have been privileged that millions have witnessed my story first-hand. Multi-millions more worldwide have experienced how I've been able to TRIUMPH OVER TRAGEDY, through the numerous television and radio interviews I've done. I didn't let a drunk driver who crashed through my house, killing my beautiful wife and seriously injuring me—stop me from communicating this message of hope.

My message is clear and simple . . . 10 seconds is all it takes to change a life forever. That is exactly what happened to me. Our lives are lived in increments of "10 second" decisions. No matter how small and insignificant each decision may seem, every single one of them will invariably have a profound impact on your life either positively or negatively. We live our lives 10 seconds at a time.

People all over America are beginning to embrace this simple life affirming action—One good decision, 10 seconds at a time. The results have been incredible! Your life can be incredible, too—but you have to take the first step. 10 seconds at a time—you will achieve your goals and dreams. Don't ever settle for less than the best.

In this book, I've compiled the very best of all the letters that have been written to me, by people just like you—real people with real stories of inspiration and triumph. They've embraced this life changing principle and are now living proof that 10 Seconds really is—changing lives forever! They are finding hope!

In my travels, there is a recurring theme that I've noticed in every single city, state, and town I've had the privilege to speak in—PEOPLE ARE LOOKING FOR HOPE. Like never before—searching for hope and courage; for something to believe in and stand for. People will always run to and bond with, whomever and whatever brings them hope. They are searching for our Purpose and Destiny. Some may think to themselves—"I've made too many bad decisions in my life—I can never change." This is not true. Even if you make a million decisions in the wrong direction—it only takes one decision, 10 SECONDS to turn your life around. You can do it.

Having been a high school coach and being a former college athlete myself, I know the value of a good coach. A good coach sees your potential and brings out the best in you. They push you to excel in ways you never thought you could before. It may not always be in sports—it can be in other talents and interests you have. I call them Life Coaches. They coach us in the importance of Life's Real Issues. Life Coaches instill in us—hope and purpose.

As you journey through this book experiencing the letters that you read and the quotes you meditate on, you too, can overcome your own adversity and find hope in everything you do. My desire above all else is that the letters contained here will bring you . . . that Hope!

I look forward to hearing from you as you begin to make good 10 Second decisions. May my experiences help coach you along your path. Visit my website and write to me and let me know: www.10seconds.org

Section 1

"Hope is a good thing—and good things never die."

Letter 1

Dear Bobby,

Yesterday, you did an assembly at my school Hatboro-Horsham High School. I have to say that it was the best assembly our school has ever had, especially on the use of drugs, alcohol, or tobacco. I sat in the front row. I was absorbing everything you said. You told the story about the girl who had shaved her head because her friend had been diagnosed with cancer and she didn't want her to go through it alone.

December 1st 1993, I was diagnosed with cancer. I went through 2 years of chemotherapy. On February 1st I had to go down to the hospital clinic for a check-up. I knew it was a big deal because on that day it had been 5 years since I had received any chemo. Before my hospital visit my best friend Meghan told me that if I ever had to go through all that again, that she would shave her head for me. I knew that if I ever had to go through all that again, that she'd do it in a second. That is all I could think about as you were telling that story and I started to cry. I don't exactly know why. I don't know if it's because that girl was such a good friend to shave her head for her friend, or because I knew that my friend would do it for me in a second. No assembly had ever made me cry before. I would just like to thank you for coming and sharing your story and others with us.

I know I wasn't the only one who was touched by your presentation. After the assembly was over almost all of my friends were asking if anyone had $5. They wanted to buy your book so much. I was lucky to find $5 and I bought "Triumph over Tragedy". I came home and left it on the table. I came downstairs later and my mom asked me if it was my book. I told her it was and she asked me where I got it. I told her I got it after the assembly she said, "Oh, cause I'm reading it now." So hopefully now my mother can also be touched and inspired by your story. Once again thank you for coming to our school.

Lauren F. , Junior at Hatboro-Horsham HS

> "The best thing you can do for your future—is live with everything you have in the present."

Letter 2

To: Bobby

My name is Dana from Tampa and I saw you at HB Plant High School in Tampa. I just wanted to thank you very much for giving that speech because it helped me to get through a very traumatizing event in January of this year. I was in a car wreck and out of 5 people, I am the only one still alive. I lost my fiancé to that wreck and am still not recovered. I broke bones and injured organs but all that is healed. I now have a titanium rod in my left femur but all that was nothing compared to the heartache I have gone through. For a long time I wanted to do nothing except die so I could be back with Tony, my fiancé, but I listened to the tape I bought—your speech and it made me realize I can do it. I can get through this and here I am e-mailing you thanking you for giving people hope in a situation that they didn't think they could find hope in. I am healed now, back in school, and trying to get back to my old life, at times it gets so hard I wanna give up but I never do. Thank you again; you don't know how much you helped me. E-mail me back when you get a chance.

Thanks again.

Dana

4

Letter 3

Date: Tuesday, September 11th, 2001, 8:15 PM EST
My name is: Kerry O., Age 29 from Stark, Louisiana
Monday, September 17, 2001 America Online: Tseconds

I wanted Bobby to know: Dear Bobby,

Today was perhaps the most tragic day in America's history. As my students watched the video footage of the World Trade Center being reduced to a pile of rubbish, my one thought was "How do you we explain this?" As a high school English teacher in a small town, I am very close to my students. It is hard to know exactly what to say to help encourage them and to help them make the right decisions. Listening to your story at our assembly today helped put things to light. I talked to many of my students and they were truly moved by your words. In a world that causes so much pain, it is so nice to see a little ray of sunshine. Thank you so much for the inspiration

Kerry O., English Teacher, Stark, Louisiana

> *"This is the moment in time—that everything you did wrong can be made right."*

> *"Courage is a choice of the heart—the more you have, the bigger your heart."*

Letter 4

Date: Thursday, January 17th, 2002
Time: 12:46 PM
My name is: Christina
I am a World Trade Center Survivor who worked on the 23rd floor.
From: Staten Island, NY
My age is: 32
I wanted Bobby to know: WOW! You are definitely an amazing man. The way you selflessly share your life with others in the hopes to motivate us to be positive and hopeful. You touched me deeply. Your wife Suzanne is also amazing I am truly happy for you both to have been blessed with love; for you a second time. I was unable to see you at the YMCA just last week (1/17/02 today). I am a World Trade Center survivor. I was at work that horrific day in Tower Two on the 23rd floor. I would rather not go into details. I am truly blessed and I have never been able to appreciate GOD so much before. Now I can actually pin

6

point every moment in my life GOD was holding my hand. My eyes have been opened wide due to the unfortunate act brought down upon America. The night of your motivational speech I was sitting next to a woman who brought her daughter. Her daughter lost her husband of three months in the World Trade Center and I couldn't stop crying for her and everyone else that wasn't as lucky as me. When you started to talk about your first love, I cried even harder. I know what 10 seconds can do to ones life. I wish my husband would learn what can happen in 10 seconds. He was with me. You see he is a drug addict. Not everyday, sometimes not even every month but he locks himself up in a hotel room and has been know to spend 2-4 days smoking crack or snorting cocaine. I had hoped beyond all hope after hearing how tragically your Ava had passed on he would stop. He has been in so many treatment programs and so many AA and CA meetings, nothing is working. You must be saying to yourself how insane I am for staying with him. But you know as well as I do that you wouldn't understand. We both attend therapy that is how we found out about you. Sometimes I think I am absolutely mad for staying with this man. But most of the time I believe whole-heartedly that God has put us in one another's lives for a reason. I think he may be my mission in life. To help him and to love him the best way I can. I have had this strong feeling especially since surviving 9/11/01 that we are together for a reason. I just haven't figured out exactly what it is yet. We love each other very much. Here's the funny thing – I don't even drink – not because I have a problem but because I choose not to. I know the horror that occur from the ignorance of others. It astounds me how many people still drink/drug and drive – what will it take for them to wake up. I could sit here and write a novel. I want to thank you for your inspiration, for sharing a very personal part of you; it was appreciated more than I can say. I hope all the young teenagers that may or may not read my story will learn; THE EASY WAY, that drinking and drugging get you nowhere in life but in trouble. You are not only hurting yourself but everyone who loves you and cares for you as well. Once you become addicted to anything your life turns upside down. Believe me you want to better yourself, go to school be happy and be a kid. Thank you for letting me share.

Christina
Staten Island, NY

Section 2

"If you keep on doing what you have been doing, you will keep on getting what you have gotten."

Letter 5

Subj: You touched my daughter's life with your kindness
Thank you, Mr. Petrocelli (and a special birthday request.)
Date: 12/27/2001
To: Tseconds
Dear Mr. Petrocelli,

My daughter Melissa heard you speak at La Plata High School in La Plata, Maryland earlier this fall. You may remember her...she is a shy, petite brunette, 16 years old, who has cerebral palsy and learning disabilities...she waited quite a long time in line to meet you and speak with you after your presentation. You were kind enough to purchase a book for her, when she realized there was a charge and she didn't have any money on her. I wanted to write and thank you for your thoughtfulness. Your kind attention to her, and the gift of your book, "Triumph over Tragedy", greatly touched her. And your story has really impacted her life. This is a child who struggles to read, and she has been patiently and diligently pouring over your book for a couple of months now (she is even reading it at meals), and is finally nearing the end. She tells me your courage in the face of adversity is inspiring to her (you may remember her telling you she has had more than 15 major surgeries in her short life...with the real possibility of more in the future). Melissa will be turning 17 years old on the 18th of January. I am mailing in an order today for a copy of "Teen Power Too", and hope to receive it in time to give it to her for her birthday gift. If

10

it were at all possible, her Dad and I would be most appreciative if you could sign a copy for her. I know she would be thrilled (as you certainly have become her hero). I would also like to take her, as well as her twin sister, to hear you speak again. Could you please have your office provide me (either by mail, or e-mail) with a list of upcoming speaking engagements, as your web site does not have this information available?

Thank you in advance, Mr. Petrocelli, for your kind attention to my request.

Sincerely,

Mary Ann M.
La Plata, MD 20646

PS...I grew up in Boston, and my father (the Superintendent of Police for the city) used to take me to Fenway Park to see your Uncle Rico Petrocelli play for the Red Sox. I especially remember their Fall 1967 season...the "Impossible Dream" team was the talk of Sacred Heart elementary school playground when I was in 5th grade...I'm sure we drove the nuns crazy with our endless discussions about Jim Lonborg, Carl Yaztremski, and #6, your Uncle Rico. Melissa got such a kick out of the coincidence that I had been a fan of your uncle, as she is of you. We marveled at life's amazing connections...your uncle touched and influenced my youth, as you have touched and influenced Melissa's.

> "Each decision you make, no matter how seemingly small, will impact your future."

Letter 6

Hi Bobby.

I am a senior at Sussex Technical High School. You visited my school yesterday, April 19, 2000. My name is Toni G. and I purchased your book, "Triumph over Tragedy." I would like to begin by telling you how much it meant for me to have the opportunity to hear your story and even talk to you one-on-one. Your story touched my heart in an unimaginable way. Now I feel like I'm not alone feeling the way I do.

My older brother Brian was in a car accident when I was in the 7th grade. The woman that he struck was killed on impact. The investigating officers ran the regular blood tests on my brother and found small amounts of THC marijuana and also alcohol from the night before in his blood. He went to trial about two years later and was found guilty of, among other charges, vehicular manslaughter. My brother was sentenced to seven years in prison. However, in his third year he was released. He came home to us last year.

As you stood out there on the floor of our gymnasium yesterday, and told us your story, I cried. I told my mom. The strange thing was, in first period yesterday a friend of mine and I were talking about my brother and I mentioned how I knew how angry and upset I felt that the other family "sent" my brother away from me. I told her I could not imagine how the other family felt since their loved one would never be coming home again and if it were my brother that had been killed how I would feel differently. Now, after hearing how you felt when you lost your loved one, I have some understanding of how that other family must have felt.

Many teens that I go to school with talk about how they get stoned and high and all, and I tell them that I don't like it. Then they ask me, "well, have you ever tried it?" I give them my usual response, "No, I've never had to do drugs to have them screw up my life. They have done enough damage to me without me needing to try it myself." Drugs played a big part in sending my brother away from us and it hurt me. I haven't seen or heard from my other brother in nearly five years. The last he called, he told my mom that if she didn't hear from him in three months, then she knew that he was dead. Bobby, I was almost 13 then and he had promised me he'd be home for my 13th birthday that April, but first he had to figure out who I was.

He was so stoned that he didn't even know me. My own brother didn't even know who I was...that hurt. I turn 18 next Tuesday. I haven't had the opportunity to share my joys with him, that I was just accepted to a college in Rhode Island or how I'm going to my senior prom in two weeks, or anything.

So, when I see people I love and care about doing that to themselves, it breaks my heart; to see that life go to waste. Thank you for visiting my school. I hope that you reached my friends more than I have been able to. I hope to get an e-mail back from you soon.

Love,
Toni G.

> *"We will always run to those who bring us hope."*

Letter 7

My name is: Ashley F. Age 17 from Leroy, NY

I wanted Bobby to know: having Bobby at our school in the little town that we call Leroy, was the most inspirational experience that I have ever experienced. While Bobby continued to tell our freshmen through senior classes about his tragic experience—it brought tears to my eyes. I wanted to go up on stage and give Bobby the biggest hug for being able to stand up there, not only this time but all the other times that he has traveled and be able to tell this story time and time again. I submitted a letter into a school contest that we had shortly after Bobby appeared at our school. Well, anyway the letter was to describe your feelings on how you thought Bobby is an inspiration to teens my age all around the world. Well, I won the contest because so much feeling and sympathy—as well as anger went into my letter. It kills me to think that anyone would want to endanger their lives as well as the lives of others. I am recently angry with my uncle because he just got a DWI for the second time after finally being able to get his license back from his underage drinking and driving experience. I just wish that bobby could reach stubborn and thick headed adults in the world that think because they live their own life—it is possible for them to do what ever they want. Even if that involves putting other people's lives at risk. I know that many teens in my school, as well as myself were very touched and thankful for Bobby to come to our school. I just want to wish him the best of luck and let him know that I think he is the best prevention for me ever letting myself or others drive drunk. Good luck, Bobby and God Bless.

Sincerely,
Ashley

"Success begins with dreams. Dreams only become reality with action."

Letter 8

Helping me see that anything is possible
Dear Bobby,

You spoke at my High School (Central Mountain High School in Mill Hall, PA) today. You changed my life within a matter of 40 minutes for the second time.

I was born with cerebral palsy which affected my legs and the way I walk. Up until 1988 I couldn't walk at all until I had a major operation to correct things somewhat. But, beyond the doctors doing the surgery, the rest was up to me.

"I'd be lying if I said it was a cake walk," which by no means it was not. It was pretty painful emotionally and physically. But, I wouldn't let myself quit no matter how bad it hurt or how frustrated I got. On September 27, 1989, it paid off and I took my first steps unaided at the age of eight.

I'm now 18 years old and a senior in High School. Over the past year I've considered almost taking my own life until I read your book. You have been the greatest blessing God could have ever given me.

I began racing cars at the age of 14 because by accident I discovered I was good at it. It became a way to escape the taunts and cruel teasing of my peers. It was somewhere where I felt safe and in control and I didn't have to please anyone but myself. But, just when I thought I would never have to cry because of another cruel remark from my peers again, it came up and slapped me right in the face.

I soon found myself the target of everyone's jokes once again, not because of my legs specifically, but because I was a girl with a disability kickin' the tar out of some of the best dirt racecar drivers in the state. It got to the point that I was going to give up just because of a little pressure. Right about then I figured I'd be nuts if I did that, and boy, was I right.

The next race I let everything just happen, no matter how upset it should have made me. During that night's race, when that curve ball came, just like the curveball that you had to deal with—I hit it right out over the fence for a grand slam home run, and I won my first race.

Reading your book and hearing you speak, made me realize that what won't kill me will only make me stronger and that life is full of curve balls...we just deal with them in the right way.

I'd like to thank you for taking the time to read my letter and giving me hope. After I won that first race, I had a special sticker made for the cockpit of my car that says, "Thanks to Bobby Petrocelli for the ten seconds that gave me—the will to live a dream." It has been there ever since and it will continue to be as long as I race. You are welcome to come and see me race sometime if you'd like. You'd be welcome on my Pit Crew any time.

Thanks for keeping the dream alive....God bless

Yours truly,
Lauren, Central Mountain High, Mill Hall, PA

TO THOSE OF YOU
To those of you who have pushed me, thank you.
Without you I would have fallen

To those of you who
laughed at me, thank you.
Without you
I wouldn't have cried.

To those of you who just
couldn't love me, thank you.
Without you I wouldn't
have know real love.

To those of you who hurt
my feelings, thank you.
Without you I wouldn't
have felt them.

To those of you who left
me lonely, thank you.
Without you I wouldn't have
discovered myself.

But it is those of you who thought I couldn't do it;
It is you I thank the most,
Because without you I
wouldn't have tried.

(Author Unknown)

Section 3

"Don't base your happiness on your circumstances. Rise above them."

Letter 9

I wanted Bobby to know: Hi Bobby~

Monday, October 15th

My name is Samantha, today you were at my High School. I bought your book and you signed it. Bobby, I just wanted to say I'm sorry about your loss, but most of all I just wanted to let you know that I admire what you are doing very much.

I know that your story really touched my heart. I'm 16 years old and my Dad has not wanted anything to do with me for the last 8 ½ years. My parents split up when I was 4, almost 5 years old. I don't remember much of it, but now what I do remember, I don't want to. My Dad is remarried and has 3 other kids. So my older sister and I aren't even in his life now unless we call or write him. He does not call or write and when we would call him he would tell us that he would call in a couple of days, but he never does. Every time he tells me that I set myself up, hoping and thinking that he's going to call. I would get so mad at him and I would stay mad at him until he called, but it would start all over again after that. My life started going down hill. All my sister, Mom and I did was fight. Mostly, because I was hurt by him and would take it out on them! All I would wonder is what I did wrong and why he didn't love me.

After hearing what you said today about forgiving people, I think I have finally realized that it's time to let go and start my life anew. Like you said—they have the problem not me! As long as I stay mad at him the longer he is going to run my life. Life is too short to be mad at him and to fight with my mom and sister. I am a Christian girl and I was always taught by my Sunday School teachers to hand my problems to God and He will take care of them, but with this I just couldn't. My Sunday School teachers tried to help me and sometimes they did, but not always. I miss my Dad very much and wish he could be here to take part in my life but he chooses not to...

I bought your book "Triumph Over Tragedy" and I'm in the process of reading it now. I've been reading it from the time I got home until now. I've enjoyed it very much so far!!!

And Bobby THANKS AGAIN!
Samantha, 16 years old, Maryland High School Student

"Each journey begins with Step 1."

Mr. Petrocelli,

My name is Billy S., I'm from Charles County, Maryland. On September 16 of this year I was on the side of the highway visiting the scene where my best friend was killed by a drunk driver. I explained to you how I was on the fire truck and responded to my friend's accident. I'm not sure if I thanked you for stopping that day or not. But know that since talking to you and reading your book things are a bit easier. My friend was taking his girlfriend home at about 11:00 PM on Sunday July 15. He was about 3 miles from his girlfriend's house and about 5 miles from his house. Justin was hit head on by a drunk driver who crossed the center line while Justin was making his way around the bend in the road. Justin didn't even have time to react I'm sure. His pick-up truck was hit head- on and flipped several times before landing on its roof, trapping him and his girlfriend inside. When I got on the scene, Justin was conscience and talking. He had very serious injuries that I was aware of because of my training as a Firefighter/EMT. I couldn't help him medically though, all I could do was kneel beside him and hold his hand and talk to him. I stayed with him all the way until he was loaded in the Med Evac helicopter and transported to Washington Hospital Center Medstar in Washington DC. A few hours later, while grieving with friends at the firehouse I was delivered the worst news I could ever imagine. A firefighter from another station who knew how close me and Justin were, broke the news to me. The way he told me will forever stick in my head as well as the mental pictures of how the scene looked and how my best friend looked while lying on the ground. For weeks I had the worst time sleeping. And for almost two and a half months there wasn't a day that went by that I didn't cry. I had lost somebody who was like a brother to me. I just recently started riding the fire truck again. When it first happened I thought for sure that I was going to take my own life or just prayed somebody else would take it for me. But the only thing that kept me going was knowing how selfish it would be of me to put everybody through the same pain all over again. I just woke up every morning wondering why I was still breathing. I visited the site of the accident every Sunday between the hours of 11 p.m. and 1 a.m. at night and several times during the week. I just knew that I was going to take my own life. I stood in the middle of the highway with my eyes closed. It was about 3 a.m. in the morning and I stood there for close to a minute but no cars came. I lucked out. I walked back to the shoulder of the road and just looked to the sky. I prayed that Justin would show me that he was up there somehow. After crying and pleading for what seemed like forever, I saw three shooting stars that were just so bright. Whether or not this was a sign from him I'll never know but I will always believe deep in my heart that it was he letting me know. Since the day after the accident I had been the closest person to Lisa. Lisa and me are now together and in some peoples eyes this is a sign of disrespect to Justin. Me and her helped each other get through the roughest times either one of us have ever faced. And a person can not help but to grow feelings for somebody whom they spend so much time with. I know that my friend would want Lisa to be happy and I know she is with me. I care so much about her that I really do not care how other people feel about it and she feels the same way about me. I told her that I would never be able to fill Justin's shoes and that it wasn't my intentions. But we both know that everybody must move on. Without her, my Mom, and your book— I think that I would still be a wreck to this day. But I have gotten back on the fire truck, am happy to wake up every morning and have found out what true love is about. I wish that I had a chance to talk to you longer. I know I wasn't very talkative when you stopped and talked to me and I don't even know if I thanked you. But Mr. Petrocelli, believe me when I say, I can't thank you enough. If you are ever in the area again please top by the Benedict Vol. Fire Department. I would like for Lisa to meet you too. Thanks so much, I know you have probably touched many lives with your talks but there is no doubt in my mind that you stopping that day, and your book have really helped me move on. Justin is in a much better place now. I still wish he was still here but at the same time I know that he was called home and he went there with his head held high. My days are brighter now and life is back to being normal just with the absence of my best friend. I know he'll be with me for the rest of my life just like your Ava will be there with you. Thanks again for your words and thoughts—they will always be remembered.

Billy S.
Captain
Bendedict V.F.D.
Maryland

Letter 11

Bobby, 10/10/2001

This is especially for Mr. Petrocelli; my deepest thanks to you for reaching out to my son, Billy S., the Benedict V.F.D. Captain here in Maryland, on September 26 up on Route 231 in Hughsville, MD. I had the privilege to hear you speak to the juniors and seniors at Thomas Stone HS recently. You are truly amazing! I think that you took the time to stop your car on the side of the road and spend time talking to Billy was incredible – Heaven sent!! He has had such an awful time trying to make sense out of his best friend's death. All of the members of VFD and Hughsville VFD have had to deal with Justin's death in their own way. These young (and not so young) people see the results of drunk drivers all too often. Again, thank you and God bless!

Ann S., Benedict, MD

> *"We can't control how others treat us, but we can control how we respond back to them."*

Letter 12

Dear Mr. Petrocelli,

My name is Katey P. and I am a senior in High School. You recently visited my school and spoke to us about making the right decisions and how in just 10 seconds your life can change forever. Your words really touched me, especially when you said that taking drugs or alcohol is like trying to catch a book when you throw it up in the air. I was dating a guy for about 6 months that I thought was really special. Then two months ago I went to the beach and when I came back I found out that he had snorted coke and cheated on me. I haven't talked to him since then, but the incident left a permanent mark in my brain and I hadn't stopped thinking about it. But when you came to speak that day, your words had so much meaning in them that I could see directed towards my incident, that I immediately felt revitalized. You were so right when you said that you "cannot control what happens to you, only how you react to it". And how sometimes that means just letting the incident go and not letting it bother you or drag it with you everywhere. You helped me to realize that things happen in everyone's life that at that time, and for that person, feel like the worst thing that could ever happen; but that's life, and you cannot control that, so you must move on and just learn from the experience. I can more easily look back at what happened with me and my ex-boyfriend, and see that I can spend the rest of my life feeling depressed that I was betrayed or I can move on and realize that he chose a path that I want nothing to do with, and so he must remain a part of my past. He was too self-centered and unmotivated to do anything for anyone but himself. And slowly that led him into a life that, unfortunately, like you said, will only keep going into doing drugs more heavily, until there will be nothing left for him to do except "drop the book". You helped me see the learning experience in all the sadness I had to deal with. I just wanted to let you know that I think you are an incredible person. While you probably read letters from high school students every day, thanking you for your wisdom, I still feel it's important for me to thank you for the influential, meaningful, and motivational words you anchored into my brain. I hope that in my future, I can find a job that is as perfect for me, as yours is for you. I hope that I am just one more small example why you should never lose faith that your words have a huge effect. I ordered your book, and am really looking forward to reading it. Thank you again and good luck.

Sincerely,

Katey P., 17 years old
High School Senior

Section 4

"Reach for your peak, your goal, your prize. It may be closer than you think."

Letter 13

Hi Bobby (I hope I can call you that), You spoke today (June 8th, Islip High School on Long Island, NY). I was very touched. I wish I could have come up to talk to you, but trying to get through the crowd and my 4th period class was too much. Plus, I admit, I didn't want to wait there and look stupid. I wanted to share a poem with you that I found somewhere on my computer. I've had it for a while and it's helped me through some things.

> Your presence is a present to the world
> You're unique and one of a kind
> Take the days just one at a time
>
> Count your blessings, not your troubles
> You'll make it through whatever comes along
> Within you are so many answers
> Understand, have courage, be strong
>
> Don't put limits on yourself
> So many dreams are waiting to be realized
> Decisions are too important to leave to chance
> Reach for your peak, your goal, your prize
>
> Nothing wastes more energy that worrying
> The longer one carries a problem, the heavier it gets
> Don't take things too seriously
> Live a life of serenity, not a life of regrets

Remember that a little love goes a long way
Remember that a lot...goes forever
Remember that friendship is a wise investment
Life's treasures are people...together

Realize that It's never too late
Do ordinary things in an extraordinary way
Have health and hope and happiness
Take the time to wish upon a star
And don't ever forget.
For even a day...
How very special you are

"Seize the moment! Today is the day you decide to get busy living or get busy dying."

Letter 14

Bobby,

   You came to my school, Robinson, today, and I wanted to let you know how much your stories affected me. I have learned to look at life from a different perspective and I am very thankful for what I have. I have heard many speakers before and you, you just reached out and touched me in a different way. I feel so horrible about what happened to you long ago, but I am glad the Lord has worked in miraculous ways to give you happiness again. I bought your "Lead Now" book with my best friend Suzanne today, and I am going to read it A.S.A.P...I am very grateful to you for speaking to us and I want you to know how many lives you have touched as well as mine today and I hope you continue speaking because you are so very wonderful at it. I am thankful to you and my life and I praise every 10 seconds of my life.

Thanks and love,

Toni M.

PS. Here's a poem I thought you would enjoy:

HOW DO YOU LIVE YOUR DASH?

I read of a man who stood to speak
At the funeral of a friend.
He referred to the dates on her tombstone
From the beginning...to the end

34

He noted that first came her date of birth
And spoke the following date with tears,
But he said what mattered most of all
Was the dash between those years (1934-1998)

For that dash represents all the time
That she spent alive on earth...
And now only those who loved her
Know what that little line is worth.

For it matters not, how much we own;
The cars—the house—the cash,
What matters is how we live and love
And how we spend our dash.

So think about this long and hard...
Are there things you'd like to change?
For you never know how much time is left,
That can still be rearranged.

If we could just slow down enough
To consider what's true and real,
And always try to understand
The way other people feel.

And be less quick to anger,
And show appreciation more
And love the people in our lives
Like we've never loved before.

If we treat each other with respect,
And more often wear a smile.
Remembering that this special dash
Might only last a little while.

So when your eulogy's being read
With your life's actions to rehash...
Would you be proud of the things they say
About how you spent your dash?

-Author Unknown

Letter 15

Dear Bobby,

My name is Jessica and I am in ninth grade at Great Neck South High School. I wrote to you a few weeks ago describing how the assembly you did, totally changed my life. My grandma was diagnosed with colon cancer about the same time I heard your inspirational speech. I was just starting to lose hope when you came in and gave me courage, strength and a new outlook for the future. Your kind words couldn't have come at a better time. After I met you, though, my situation took a turn for the worse. My grandma couldn't find a doctor who would take her insurance coverage, and she was so scared. My mother also had a gallbladder attack and spent the night in the hospital. Things just started to cool down now, but there are two surgeries that face my family. My mom is getting her gallbladder removed tomorrow, and my grandma is getting her cancer operation the following Monday. Since the tragedies that struck my family, I have had the opportunity to try to escape by other means, however, I choose not to. Your bravery and power have also added to my decision to face the world, and not run away from my problems. There hasn't been a day that does by, that I haven't thought about you at least once. I think about what you had to go through, and how you triumphed over it. I derive strength from your positive message and now I know that I am not grieving alone. I refer to you as my angel, because you are truly someone sent from up above. No matter what life throws at me, I know now, that I can face it. Thank you for being who you are. I am so glad you had another chance at happiness and that you have a wonderful family.

God Bless,

Jessica, Long Island, NY

> *"Before we can believe in others, we have to believe in ourselves."*

Letter 16

Dear Mr. Petrocelli,

I am writing to you because I was in the assembly you spoke to at Washingtonville High School, I am a senior and you touched my heart greatly! I wanted to buy your books but I had no money on me, it was very upsetting, I actually went all the way home after your assembly to get money but by the time I got back to school no one was there. If you could please give me a list of books you've written so that I could purchase them I would appreciate it. Also I just wish you could talk to everyone especially my sister, I love her dearly but she went through a tough ordeal about five years ago and I think she still carries it on her back. She had a hair condition where every time she had a high temperature, all her hair would fall out, Unfortunately she got sick in seventh grade and lost all her gorgeous blonde hair, so naturally she tried to go to school with a wig on but the students were so horrible to her, they made fun of her and pulled off her wig. She was so embarrassed that she had to be home tutored for an entire year while her hair grew back. Ever since she has had a negative attitude about people. She always looks to the bad side of things and has become very miserable about life. I can't remember her being happy about anything since. I think she just needs to forgive people and let it go. I think if she listened to your speech she would start to look on the brighter side of things and enjoy life. Mr. Petrocelli, not only did God save you the day of your tragedy but he made you an angel – a human guardian angel! You are a savior and I thank God for letting me have the opportunity to be touched by you. I am looking at things differently now, the way I should have all along. You are very good at your job; I've never seen my class give a standing ovation before I see now that they were saving it for the best performance – you. Thank you so much for what you did for me today, and for what you are making everyone else see. I think that I have the strength to help my sister, I will let her read your books, and I will try to show her what you showed me. I hope that you keep talking to kids, they need to get the message and you gave it to us in a way we would understand. You won my respect in "ten minutes", and I'm sure changed every life in that auditorium as well. I would love to go on and tell you about myself and how you've made me think differently but I know if I do you'll never get to see your boys. I can't thank you enough. Also could you please give me a list of your books, I want to be able to help people to, and give them the knowledge you've given me. Thank you again, you are a true Angel!

Sincerely,

Roberta F.

> # "She ain't heavy, she's my sister."

Section 5

"When life throws you a curveball, you can hit it."

Letter 17

Dear Mr. Petrocelli,

My name is Heidi and I'm and English teacher in Tampa, Florida. My fifth period class had the privilege of attending your presentation in March. I apologize for the time it has taken to sit down and finally write this letter; things have been crazy with quarter grades due and new classes starting up. However, despite the time that has lapsed, I wanted to take some time and write to you to extend my thanks and to let you know how much I admire and respect what you do.

Personally, I am in awe of the inner strength you have had to overcome your tragedy. You spoke, in your presentation, about the "curve balls" that life throws us- and it certainly threw you a large one-but you were so right in saying that you smacked it right out of there, and that it's still going. You are truly an inspiration. Your story is not only a testament to the power of humanity to rise above tragedy, but it is also a reminder to us all that we DO have a responsibility to one another. In so many ways, life is a series of cause and effect relationships; one never really knows the extent to which one's actions may affect others—others who may not even be immediately in our lives. The class that attended your presentation had just finished reading Arthur Miller's <u>The Crucible</u>. One of the major themes that we looked at was the issue of social responsibility - examining just when and where-if ever-our obligations to those around us stop or start. We had some pretty deep moments of realization/discussion as we looked at the choices characters made—some motivated by greed and self-gain, others by concern for others-but it was still distanced from "real life" for my kids. Your story was the perfect "real life" illustration for my kids to really see that point hit home. I've often tried to explain that concept to my students with the following analogy: The actions and choices we make are life pebbles that we drip into a pool of water. That act of dropping that pebble into the water sends out an initial ripple, that creates another ripple, and the pattern continues infinitely, until the last one touches land. So, the pebble-which never was thrown directly at or perhaps was never even intended to affect the land—in fact, DOES affect it, even if it is not an immediate result. Your story reminded me of that quite clearly.

As educators, you and I are quite familiar with the pressures that teens face as well as the sense of invulnerability some of them carry. In speaking with my students after your presentation, they really feel that you understand those pressures, and I know that many of them were sincerely touched by your words—and, perhaps, have become a bit more aware of their own vulnerability and/or of the fact that they CAN affect others with the choices they make.

I have seen several copies of your book in the hands of students across campus, so I know that many of them are still thinking about your words. I purchased your books, also, and I have them up on a shelf at the front of my room. Just about every day, in just about every class, someone is using before/after class time to look through them...or reading through them when he/she is finished with his/her work. Many have asked for your email address, as well. You certainly have left your mark on many of the students here at our school—and you have certainly left your mark on me. Personally, I know your story has made me re-examine some of my priorities as well as reaffirm my belief that we all DO have an obligation to "look out for" one another.

I just wanted to let you know that your words were well received and very valuable. I am glad that, in your busy schedule, you were able to share your message with those of us here in Tampa. Enclosed you will find a few letters by some of my students who wanted to thank you too. I told them that I was going to write you a letter, and that I would be happy to include any of theirs with mine…so they are included as well. Thank you again, and I send my best wishes to you and your family.

Sincerely,
Heidi Q., English Teacher, Tampa, FL

"A kind word is like a cool drink of water, and refreshes everything it touches."

Letter 18

Mr. Petrocelli,

I have been a victim of depression for over five years, but was only diagnosed last year. I have been through a lot, from being made fun of in school to watching my grandfather die from a massive stroke at age twelve. It is hard to describe how I felt all those years. At first it wasn't too bad. I thought of myself as a big, fat, ugly failure in fifth grade, but it grew bigger; I got to where I saw nothing good about myself at all. I was suspicious of everyone. I thought to myself, "No one likes me, they're just nice to me because they feel sorry for me, they just don't want me to know how hideous I am." I would cry for hours on end, those hard sobs that makes your body shake and you can't breathe, for hours sometimes. I would get so angry with myself I would enter this black place, where I didn't know what I was doing. I began causing self-inflicted wounds to myself, I had bruises, scratches and everything, but when I did it I was so mad I couldn't feel it. I thought, "Hey, let's give everyone reason to think I am this ugly creature, I'll make myself look like one." There were several times I would be crying and so upset that I would black out almost. One minute I would be in my room crying, the next thing I knew I was in the bathroom with a razor blade touching my wrist. Luckily I always snapped together before it was too late. This dark stage went on for about two years before I decided I couldn't take it anymore. I now am on medication to replace the seratonin in my brain. I have never admitted being suicidal to anyone before because it scares me to think I was that way. Don't get me wrong, everyday is still a struggle and some are worse than others are, but I am gradually learning to deal with who I am. I am going to be a senior this year and I never would have made it if I had killed myself. I am embarrassed by my condition, but at the same time I'm proud of myself for holding on. You are an angel sent from Heaven here to help me and others like me live life feeling free, confident, but also think about their decisions. I am eternally grateful and can never say thank you enough.

Thank you once again for all you have done,

Katie L.

> *"An investment in helping others is more precious than diamonds and gold."*

Letter 19

May 22nd

Dear Mr. Bobby Petrocelli,

It is now precisely 10:39 p.m. (so says my girly alarm clock) and I am writing you because I am the type of person that cannot sleep when I have things on my mind. My name is Meghan Elizabeth P. and I am turning 17 on the 30th of this month. I wanted to first tell you a little bit about myself. You came to give a speech today at my school, Wamogo Regional High School in Litchfield, CT and I want you to know that I was moved more than words can say. Let me explain to you a little why. Now, I must say, I don't have a story remotely near yours because I've never lost a loved one so dear to me and I don't have as strange coincidence relating to knowing you but you still touched me emotionally and warmed my soul. I'm not originally from Connecticut or anywhere near here, in fact. I was born in California and moved here from there last year to live with my father. I was living in East Los Angeles with my mother and all of my family and I just made a decision to move with my father who was previously abusive to my mother and myself. It was a mistake.

To make a long story short, he was ten times as abusive and he didn't change like I had thought when I moved here. I am presently in a foster home in Winsted. This has been the most difficult thing for me to adjust to and I've been through a lot. It was the most difficult decision I had to make on my own. I'm aware of how much courage it took. But, I did it and I am no longer in danger. But, let me tell you, it's not at all easy for me to go to school in this small, country school when I'm used to being a minority in my old Los Angeles schools. And not only did I have to deal with that change, but I had my personal situation on top of it – actually – I do right now. When you spoke today about cruelty in young people like myself and how there's no respect etc., I wanted to run up there and hug you because I felt like you understand me. I've been a victim of cruelty all my life and I've learned positive ways to deal with it, thanks to my wise mother who taught me to rise above their level. But, point is, especially at this school, cruelty is a big problem and I, to this day, have to deal with mean people. Even when the cruelty is not directed at me it affects me. I'm not used to this negativity all the time. Anyway, I wanted to thank you personally for your speech because it did make a huge difference in my life because it showed me that there are people out there somewhere that care and understand and who are good people and that you can take a negative experience and turn it into something good that can hopefully make other people's lives better. You see, I was hoping that I could speak someday at battered women's shelters and write a book of my own about my life (because it gets much more complicated than what I briefly told you) and help girls (and boys) just like me so that I, too, can make a difference. I can tell it's a good feeling to make a difference just to help people – that it's a satisfaction beyond money – I could read that satisfaction on your face when you finished today. And the beauty of it is – every time you speak, you help yourself as well as others.

So, in closing, please know that you did make a difference in my life today.

Sincerely,

Meghan Elizabeth, High School Student, CT

P.S. You also showed me that there are decent guys out there who aren't violent. When I got home today – no lie – I listened to the tape I bought of your college address – the whole thing – and I'm glad I did because I now know that if ever I'm down, I can pop that tape in and make myself feel better. You're an angel, and you're right – you did survive for a reason, to share your gift. I'm also looking forward to reading your book that you signed for me today. So God bless you, sir!!

(P.S. To add a touch of humor as you do so well in your speeches, you also showed me that you New England people aren't so bad – you're kinda cool, actually! So, when I go back home to Los Angeles this summer, I can say I met an all right New Yorker!!)

Take care and thanks for taking the time to read it all! I wish you and your family the best, thank you.

Letter 20

Bobby-

I had the privilege to listen to you speak at the Montana BPA State Convention last week, last year at another assembly. But last week was the first time I truly listened. What you said I know had tremendous impact on those from my school. In fact, I read your entire book "Triumph over Tragedy" on the bus ride home and my friends are now sharing it.

I belong to what some may consider the "in" crowd at my school, where it's almost like you feel pressured constantly to uphold some sort of image-being confident, no insecurities, no staying home on the weekends-going to parties instead. Sometimes I would just like to turn off the phone and hang out in my room. After your assembly, I went back to my hotel room (also shared by three of the other popular girls at my school) and I think we all knew what each other was feeling. As soon as the door shut, we just sat on our beds and cried. In all the times that we did awful things like drinking, we never stopped to think about whom we could have hurt. Fortunately, we made a pact right then and there to always think about what you said before making any rash decisions. I now carry your "10 Seconds" sticker in my purse, and anytime I open it I am reminded of the selfless gift that you offer to help so many others. I can only imagine the pain you must feel each time you step on stage. Thank you for caring so much for others that you are willing to put everything you hold dear on the line in hopes of making a difference. You have.

God Bless,

MJ, Age 16, Montana

> "Change your circumstances by changing your attitude."

Section 6

"Love may be lost, but never lose love. Hope may seem lost, but never lose hope—it is always there."

Letter 21

About my daughter, Christy

To: Bobby Petrocelli

Hello, my name is Paulette. I spoke with you over the phone this past September. I hope you remember. My daughter Christy was killed June 9th, right after graduating from high school. You spoke at her High School in May here in Amherst, Ohio. I told you that she had purchased your book, and you signed it for her. You asked me to tell you about her and to send you a picture of her so that you could place it in your office. When we spoke, you were on your cell phone on your way to, I do believe you said Louisiana, to speak at a high school there. You had asked me if it would be all right to mention "Christy from Ohio", in your speech. I said yes. Do you remember?

Well I truly apologize that I haven't been in contact with you. I've been trying to deal with this and it's been a struggle for me. I want you to know that. So, here I am. I'd like to share something with you.... . Today is the 12th; eight months ago today we buried her. I was in her room a bit ago, just looking at her closet full of clothes and just missing her so very much. Once again, there was your book. (That's the exact same thing that prompted me to contact you back in September, your book!) So as I was flipping through the pages, there was an insert, like a large postcard. I looked on the back and there was your email address. Now Bobby, this had happened twice!!!!! I feel Christy wanted me to contact you again, cause it's this feeling I'm getting.

Christy loved BUTTERFLIES!!!

Well I must go for now, I'll look forward to hearing from you. I check messages throughout the day.

Take care,
Paulette, Amherst, OH

> *"No matter what you've done and how far you've gone astray, it only takes 10 Seconds to turn yourself around and put your life on the right path."*

Letter 22

Bobby,

Hey man...You just came to our school and you really moved me...You said that 10 seconds could change your life forever and that we should stop the drugs and alcohol abuse right now because life is like a curve ball and you have to learn how to swing the bat of life and knock it our of our way to go on and lead a better life. I have been abusing my self with drugs and alcohol and it has gotten me into a lot of trouble. I didn't think it was hurting anyone but all the while...I was hurting me and my family. You don't really realize that until it hits you like a ton of bricks...The very day that you came to our school which was the 18th day of May I had been clean for about 2 months...I was really confused and was in a position where I had lost friends from the things that I had done and the only way to get them back was to hold my head up...So the very next day as I walked into school...I held my head up, I knew I was a good person now and that I could change my life...The whole day I had this feeling that was filled which was before empty...It felt great and my life from that point on I knew would be better off. Thank you for inspiring me to lift up my head...It only took 10 seconds to realize you only live once and that doesn't mean go party and do drugs...It meant live your life to the fullest and do the right things...and that is what I plan to do and what I am doing now...Thank you very much...You will be on my list of prayers now...

Steve
Pennsylvania

Letter 23

I wanted Bobby to know—I just want to say what you do is very inspirational. Let's say last year was the " year from hell" for me. I ran away 3 times, was always fighting with my Mom, I probably have 5 dozen holes in my stomach from trying to commit suicide, and I was eventually put in a mental hospital for a while. After a while I realized things had to change. It is taking a while but it getting better even though I know my depression will never fully go away. I have learned that the people I was with were not the best and the things that I was doing weren't so good either. Since this epiphany I have noticed what gifts God gave me and I am starting to put them to use. When you came to Donegal and you told your story and read your book I knew exactly what you went through. I was in amazement in how you told your story without falling apart like I often do. All I know is that I want to help the world in any way I can whether it is singing or writing poetry to tell people that there is always a way out. You have touched me a lot and I wish the best for you and your family. God bless you and remember that you will always have the people who you've touched to fall back on when times get rough.

Julie S., Mount Joy, PA

"What you can be is more important than what you have done."

Letter 24

Hi Bobby!

My name is Jana. I am a High School student from LA, where you spoke this morning. I couldn't wait to get home to my computer so that I could write to you. I was extremely impressed by your talk. You see, on January 31 of this year, I was brutally attacked and raped in my own home by my neighbor's boyfriend who is 29 years old. At the time, I was 16. I fought with all my strength and put my trust in God to get me through that terrifying 1½ hours. I honestly believe I would not be here without Jesus Christ. Over the past nine months, I have been dealing with anger, stress and many other painful emotions. The court battle has put so much stress on me, and it's still not over. I am afraid that I will go through my entire senior year (this year) dealing with court. I just want to be a normal teenager. But, the reason that I am writing to you is first of all to thank you for coming to my school today. My day started off very stressful, and you brightened it up. You also made me decide what I wanted to do to help people who may be in the same situation I was put in. I want to travel and tell people about my experience. I want to let them know that there are people who care about them and it is not at all their fault. Thanks so much for being there today.

Love,

Jana
MAY GOD BLESS YOU, SUZANNE, ALEC & ARON!!!!
Please write back. It would mean a lot to me. Thanks!!!

Section 7

"The tongue can cut sharper than any blade, and more harmful than any weapon. Use it to build up rather than tear down."

> # "Pay attention to what's important, not what's impertinent."

Letter 25

Hi Bobby,

You spoke at my school today. I just wanted to say that no one has ever affected me like you had today. A few weeks ago I found out that my 19-year-old sister was pregnant. Obviously, my house is in total chaos. Throughout constant arguments my sister and I have been I guess ganging up on my mom. You made me think about some of the things that we've been saying to her. They are definitely things that if I was a mother it would make me think twice about even having a reason to be on this earth. I just wanted to thank you for making me think of my words, I would never be able to forgive myself if something happened to her because of me. You are I'm sure, an inspiration to many people, including me.

Thank you.
Melissa
Long Island, NY

Letter 26

Hello. This is Brian D., a student, that saw your assembly on April 14th and I thought that you had the best motivational speech skills that I have ever seen. You were really funny, and right to the point, which really gets through to kids my age. I have Attention Deficit Disorder better known as ADD, but because I have this disorder sometimes I have a hard time paying attention and often I am "off task" as most of my teachers put it, but when you were talking in the assembly it wasn't hard to focus about what you were saying I was always on the edge of my seat ready to hear what you were going to say next, the things you said really stuck in my mind like about 10 seconds can change your life and about the terrible accident (that I'm sorry about) and the part about learning from your past. If all my teachers knew how to speak and get across the idea as well as you I know that my grades would be better. Thanks for speaking at our school!!!

Sincerely, Brian D.

> *"Rising above your circumstances means reaching beyond your perceived limitations."*

Letter 27

These are my comments:

Bobby- I just wanted to take 10 seconds out of my life to thank you from the bottom of my heart for speaking at our school. I never realized half of what you said until you said it tonight. I realize that forgiving the people that stripped me of any self-esteem, pride and feeling of safety was the best thing I could do for myself. See, two years later I was raped. I was and am too scared to tell anyone so I deal with it by myself. I was once again raped last spring, almost a year ago. Coping with this and the molestation that occurred in my childhood sent me places that I wish I never would have went, but I did and with your assembly I realized that I can put them in the past and leave them there and the best thing I could do is forgive these people and move on with my life because they are just brining me down. I now see that the bad things in my life have made me a stronger person. I just needed someone to give me the courage to believe in myself again and made me feel like a whole person. And you did this! I will pray for you tonight when I go to bed Bobby and thank God for bringing you here to Iowa and showing me the brighter side to life. Any family should thank God every night for letting you be part of their lives because you Bobby are truly a special, special person. I am sorry you had to go through what you did just to send your message across the United States, but God does everything for a reason. Again, I thank you from the bottom of my heart and no longer will I cry myself to sleep because I hurt, but now because I am thankful for my life and all that is in it.

Thank you so much again, may God bless you and your family always-I'll keep you in my heart forever-

Katie E.
Storm Lake, Iowa

> "In order to triumph you must first begin with try."

Letter 28

Mr. Petrocelli,

Hello, my name is Tom H. I am an eleventh grade student in Pennsylvania. I am e-mailing you to thank you for coming to our school last week and talking. I found your presentation very impacting and I believe that so did a lot of our school. There have already been less fights and arguments among my fellow classmates, and many are starting to realize that drinking is stupid, especially under age! There have been a lot less parties being planned, at least with alcohol available to them.

I will tell you a little about me and how I found your presentation very helpful. I am a firefighter right now with a nearby fire department. I have gone on many wrecks where people have been badly hurt or killed due to DUI's. Most being people not even involved with alcohol. Ever since you spoke to us I also have started taking many more precautions, such as stabilizing a vehicle. I finished reading your book, "Triumph over Tragedy", the other day. I now carry it with me to calls. I ordered another one of the same book. I am going to lend your book to families who loose someone close to their heart. I read a little of your book to my mother's friend. She lost her husband last year due to a drunk driver. The entry I read to her, "Will I ever live again?" brightened not only her day, but she now has the power to go out more. She wanted to also thank you.

This may seem kind of strange, but when I get older I want to be a paramedic. I like helping others. Your book made me think a lot especially about life and death situations, but I think I still want to follow my dreams. I think that I have a solid foundation already.

I just want to thank you once again for sharing your story with us! Take care, God bless! If you get a chance in your busy life feel free to reply to me, but if not I understand completely!

You are my new idol! Thanks for your support, even though you may not know you supported me, but your book says it all!

Good-bye friend,
Tom H., PA

> *"In life, pain is inevitable, suffering is optional."*

Section 8

"Get out of someone's shadow and back into the sunlight—your own light will shine brighter than ever."

Letter 29

Dear Bobby,

I am writing this email because I wanted to let you know how much of an impact that you have made in my life. The first time I heard you speak was at my High School in Pennsylvania. Now I must admit that sometimes I don't always go into these types of assemblies with the right attitude. But I must tell you, when I left after your presentations, I left with something that touched my heart. I guess is should start by introducing myself.

My name I Elizabeth and I am 17. I am now a junior in High School. I play soccer, and have been on the varsity team since freshman year. That is an accomplishment that I am very proud of. I also play softball for a club team during the summer. I am involved in choir Legacy (the select vocal group) the all-school musical, Jr./Sr. class play, student council and I am a class officer for my class of 2002. One thing you might not be expecting is the fact that I am also a self-mutilator. So many people have told me before that I have so much going for me that they don't understand what could make me want to hurt myself. And sometimes I don't even have a reason.

It started my freshman year and continued for years. It began as a simple scratch and eventually caused me to bleed for hours. I wanted so badly to fit in and be wanted that I caused myself extreme amounts of stress. I set unrealistic goals for myself and expected them to be reached even though deep down I knew it was impossible. I compared myself to my older brother who in my eyes was so much smarter, more popular and a better athlete. I wanted to be like him; someone everyone knew and loved and someone others respected. I thought that if I didn't reach his status, then I wasn't worth it. I pushed myself too hard at everything I did. I wanted to be the best at everything and never settled for less. If I didn't succeed, then I would cut myself as some sort of punishment. The pain helped me in some way. When I saw the blood, it was like all my problems were flowing out with it. I know it sounds sick, but it was truly the way I felt. I went to parties with my brother and hung out with an older crowd. I was introduced as "Jimmy's little sister" and from then on, I had the status and popularity that I wanted so badly. Making the school musical and Legacy, as well as the varsity team only added to this desire for perfection. At these parties were the usual, beer, mixed drinks and weed. Thinking I had to do this stuff to "look good" I joined in. What I didn't realize was that not everyone really was doing it, including my brother. The first time he caught me, he couldn't believe what I did, and he took me home and talked to me about it. That was the first time that I had told him or anyone about the cutting. I explained that I wanted to be like him and I wanted to be perfect. He told me that I already was and that doing this to myself wasn't going to make any difference. Over the next couple of months things got a little better, but I would still suffer from spurts of relapse into cutting. Then I heard you speak for the first time.

I thought that your story was the most influential story that I had heard in a very long time. I cannot imagine going through what you did, and then going on with your life to succeed the way you have. I admire your strength and courage. I listened to you that day and I knew that if you could overcome something as tragic as the loss of your wife, and the injuries you had on your body, then I could overcome my sense of self-hatred. You had to work past so many emotional setbacks, and in a way, I felt that you and I related. You had to reach inside to find the will to move on with your life and realize your strengths. I had to do the same. I had to stop hating myself and accept myself for the wonderful girl I am. Another thing that really shook me up was the pictures I saw of your injuries. You had endured so many physical hardships and injuries. I am sure that nothing would ever want to make you relive your pain. I looked at you and then looked at myself in disgust. There I was causing my own self and pain and injury. Now I know that they weren't of the same manner, but you see what I'm getting at? You talked about the ten seconds that changed your life. Let me tell you about the ten that changed mine. It was the ten seconds that it took me to sit down with my brother by my side and look my parents in the eye and tell them that "Mom and Dad, I have been hurting myself mentally and physically and I need help." That was it. They got me the help that I needed and I am so much better now. It took a lot of therapy and tears to get to the root of the problem, but once we discovered it, it was like a ton of bricks had been taken off my shoulders. I would have never had the courage to talk to my parents without your encouragement. Your story was one that really touched my life. I recently heard you speak again at the Holiday Inn in York. It was at the alcohol and drug conference. I really wanted to come up to you in person and tell you all of this, but time didn't allow it. I also wanted you to know that since my recovery, I have refused to touch a drug or alcoholic beverage. I am finally able to see that I really do have a lot going for me, and that I am a good person and can do anything that I put my mind to. You chose to succeed in life when it threw you a curve ball. You didn't give up. That's what I did too. I have not cut in over a year and I am so proud to tell you this. I have the best friends and the best family that anyone could ask for, and that's all that really matters. I achieved the "status" I wanted by being myself and not being fake. I just wanted to thank you for sharing your story with my school and with so many other schools around the country. I wouldn't be where I am today if it weren't for your inspiration! I would like if you would just drop me a note back to let me know that you read my letter; but I understand your time schedule, and will be happy just to know I sent you the letter!

Thank you!
Much love and respect
Elizabeth W., PA

> "If you just stop and think—and take it slow, the truth will come to you and be more clear than crystal."

Letter 30

This is Brian R.,

I sat for an hour and watched as Mr. Petrocelli poured his heart out to a gymnasium full of one thousand 14-18 year old students about the heartbreak, and upset, and tragedy of his story. And then, I watched as our administrators filed students aggressively and forcefully out of the gym.

I saw torn faces. I saw tears. I saw heads hanging and people searching for answers. The answers could be found in the man who opened himself up in front of an entire high school, and left a piece of his heart

Your friend,
Brian R., Student, Long Island, New York

p.s. The time it will take for this to get from my computer to yours is probably around ten seconds. Another ten seconds. Tonight I wrote a song, a short song inspired by you and your story. I want to share it with you, and you can feel free to share it with whomever else you feel like.

You never think,
What could go wrong?
In a time,
Ten seconds long.
Your life could change,
You'd never know,
If you just stop,
And think and take it slow.

A title of that song is Ten Seconds. Thank you again from the very bottom of my heart and soul. And I wish you the best of luck, and life. To Alec, and Aron, and Suzanne. Thank you very much.

> *"Forgiveness is a conscious decision that will set you free today."*

Letter 31

Dear Bobby,

Hi! My name is Dana F., I am 16 years old, and I am a very active board member of SADD at my High School in Westchester, NY. I attended the assembly at Fox Lane High School on April 5. I don't know if you remember me but I was the brown haired girl in the tan skirt that could not stop crying!!! Thanks for your hugs and sweet words.

I wanted to let you know that everything you said, I could connect with in one way or another, and I know others that were sitting at my table felt the same way. **You struck us all to the core**, and it was amazing. So many things you told us about growing up, and how to forgive, and how lots of teenagers are shallow and can hurt us, but we should let go of it because we won't know them years from now...are things that I have figured out in my mind...but just never saw them clearly until you said it. Your entire speech, or lecture, or whatever you want to call it, was phenomenal. I am sure you hear that quite often.

I doubt you have time but I would like to tell you a little bit about myself because you seem like an open person who is in love with life.

Well back in November of this past year, I got into a car accident. What happened was I was at a party with all my friends and I knew for some reason that I shouldn't drink that night because I felt something bad was gonna happen...but I stayed there anyway. Then it was time to leave this kids house so we all decided to meet at the nearest elementary school so that we could figure out what we wanted to do from there. Of course I have this friend, Brian, who thinks he is invincible. He drives drunk ALL THE

TIME. All summer long, and even up until that November. Anyway, a lot of the kids piled into his car. He had a jeep. I decided there was no way I was about to get into his car...So I grabbed my friend Michelle out of Brian's car (because she was inebriated and didn't know the difference) and I called my friend Josh to come pick us up and bring us with them over to the elementary school to make sure they were okay. Long story short...as we were leaving the school Brian decided to drive like an idiot and start swerving...he crashed into Josh' car. I was in the passenger side. The only damages done were to myself and my ex-boyfriend who was in the passenger side of Brian's car. We both got our knees banged up pretty badly.

It could have been worse, but I was shaken by the entire thing. If we were going faster than about 20 mph I could have banged my head on the windshield of Josh's little Neon and died. AND FOR WHAT REASON?! I thought I did all the right things by getting a designated driver, not drinking that night, grabbing Michelle out of Brian's car because I was looking out for a friend. **It all blew up in my face.**

Anyway...Then, my best friend thought she got pregnant by her 21-year-old boyfriend. I tried to help her and tell her to stay away from him...but she is too weak, I cant' even look at her these days. She is pathetic and it makes me sick. Also, my friend Matt who is sophomore got arrested for having weed in school, he isn't a bad kid, he just made a stupid choice.

I try to help my friends out as much as I can, but it seems like entire school is just corrupt. But I guess it is like that everywhere. I don't even hang out with the "druggies" or any of that, my group is "fairly popular, gets good grades" crowd. So no one would ever know the crap I have to deal with. I am not saying I am all-good. I call people names if they call me names first, you taught me just to let it go. I have been told that my entire life, but you made it all finally make sense. THEY AREN'T WORTH MY TIME!

I know this E-mail is lengthy but hang on…I just have about two more stories to tell you…and I'll be finished! I told my student's assistance counselor about Brian's drunk driving and about how my ex-boyfriend would drink ALL the time and that is the only time he was nice to me, and that he wouldn't open up and talk unless he was "under the influence." So anyway, I told her about hem because I CARED about them, not because I was a rat. They took it the wrong way…basically forced it out of me to tell them that I was the one who had told on them. Then all my friends started calling me a "stupid bitch" and were like "I can't believe you did that, if they had a problem we would know and we would have said something to someone, you always have to butt into other people's business," BUT, if I was butting into someone else's business, I would have done something else and told a teacher, or a parent, or all the kids in the school, which I easily could have. Instead, I decided to tell a counselor confidentially because it was on my conscience and again…**IT BLEW UP IN MY FACE!**

I stopped caring about people for a while, I felt I had lost all my "true" friends and **I hurt everyone else who was there for me** and who were my actual real friends and who cared about ME.

I had become NUMB. Al I wanted was to feel and love again but I just didn't trust anyone because everything, no matter what, blows up in my face eventually. I guess **you taught me to feel and care again,** that is why I cried so hard, but I just want to **thank you with all my heart.** It was

a cry well needed! And, I am sorry for all the terrible things you had to go through because of one stupid person and ten seconds! But you turned out to be amazing and you really have affected lives...so thank you.
Much love,
 Dana F.
Westchester, NY
PS...You probably don't hear this much because you are always saying it to everyone else...but... "you are beautiful!"
PPS...If you get a chance, please write back. It doesn't have to be long!

> ## "Be willing to wait for the Payoff."

Letter 32

You were Sooooo Inspirational...

Hey Bobby,
   Thank you sooooo much for coming to my High School in Erie, PA. You really left us all amazed. Even if some of the students were ignorant enough to skip or not take your lesson to heart, you really touched me. I am not one of those students who have a lot of problems at home...but I do have it kinda rough....I grew up without my real biological father. My mom was only 17 when she gave birth to me and my father wanted her to get an abortion. Well, she refused to so he didn't want anything to do with me. To this very day he still doesn't. I have a wonderful stepfather now, but part of me feels really empty knowing that my flesh and blood is walking around somewhere in town not having a care in the world about his daughter that he left behind. I know I am probably better off without him, but I am at this stage in my life where I need my father. I feel like there is a part of my heart missing. A piece of the puzzle that is lost. Like I said, I am not one of those teenagers that have problems in the home (and I thank God for that every day), but there is still that part of me that feels like I wasn't good enough for my own father. Like I was some sort of disgrace. I know that I am not, but being a teenager in this day and age, it is really hard to think otherwise. I just keep telling myself that he is the one missing out and in the end I will be a better person.

I just wanted to THANK YOU soooooooo much for coming to talk to us. I really have never felt so close to someone I don't know. Thank again for everything and keep up the great work.

Oh and I know that when our Lord Jesus Christ decided that it was time for Ava to come home, He wasn't ready to take you because He had this all planned for you and I could not be more THANKFUL...

I wish you and your family a lifetime of happiness and may God Bless you in every way, shape and form.
You truly are an Angel.

With Lots of Love,
Andrea H., Erie, PA

P.S. I hope that other students can experience everything that I experienced this very day. Thanks to you, I see a different light. I Love You!!!!

Section 9

"Many wonderful things will never get done if YOU don't do them."

Letter 33

Dear Bobby,

    I have recently seen you speak at my High School in New York. Despite that fact I was sitting in the front row and you spit on and pointed at me, I got your message loud and clear, and almost, and almost brought me to tears. My whole life has been entangled with drug and alcohol abuse. My youngest brother, who is 15 years older than me and is now 30, was a drug and alcohol abuser for 6 years. It ripped our family apart having him in jail and the pain of knowing or thinking at least, that my parents had done something wrong, or had failed him, disputes came about and my parents, married for 25 years divorced. But me being only a small child, this had no effect on me until I started to see myself going in the same direction. I believe that when children hear stuff over and over from their parents they do not fully believe it. And I have heard these stories throughout my life. My family has a long history of alcohol abuse, so there is a psychological inheritance. My mother has always warned me about it might happen for me, but I didn't believe her, and I totally regret that. I had started to drink and it became a game for me. I didn't know the real pain I could be putting myself and others around me in. My brother (now sober for 7 years) saw it happening to me and begged me to stop, but children of my age, know everything and I ignored him. My boyfriend also saw it, and hated it very much. It took almost losing the 2 things that mattered most to me (my brother and my boyfriend)

84

to think about what my priorities were. My family and love or drinking. I now see that in making this decision I did the best thing for everyone around me, including myself. Even though you only talked to us today, I hold you partially responsible for this. I thought long and hard after you left about all the things you said how one 10 second decision could change everything. I believe the commitment I made to myself today; my "10 Second Decision" that I made during your speech this afternoon will change my world for the better. My boyfriend, family and I have you to thank for our happiness to come. Thank you Bobby!!

I am so glad that you came to speak to us. You are truly an inspiration to us all for picking up your life the way you did. More people should think optimistically like you rather than giving up on the world.

~Sincerely,
~Deborah F., Age 16, Sophomore, Upstate, NY

> *"No matter what you've been through, there is someone else who can totally relate to your situation."*

Letter 34

Monday, April 16th
I wanted Bobby to know: Bobby,

I was at Safe Spring, at Skidmore College, when you spoke to us. Your speech was very inspirational. I can totally relate to what you said about the girl who had cancer. When I was in the third grade, I was diagnosed with Acute Lymphocytic Leukemia. I came back to school and I was picked on for being bald and kids ripped my hat off my head. It was humiliating. However, my classmates helped me a lot, the school had fundraisers to help raise money for the American Cancer Society. You really caught my attention at that assembly. Thank you so much and I would love to help in any way to possibly spread the message to kids about making the right decisions.

Take care, with lots of love,
Ashley, Waterford, NY

"Your life is valuable. You are alive for a reason. You will find your purpose and destiny."

Letter 35

I wanted Bobby to know:

December 31, 1984 the day I was born I was a miracle
and didn't even know it. I was 10 weeks (2 ½ months)
premature. To be born 10 weeks early and at 4lbs I was
either facing death or to be damaged in one way or
another for life. Lucky for me I am fine and in working
condition. But then on December 29, 2000 I was in a car
accident and flown to Shock Trauma Baltimore. We were
going down a straight road and a driver swerved into our
lane making us hit the brakes and swerved to the right
hitting the guardrail. When trying to recover we went to
the left and hit another guardrail ripping through it
hitting a ditch and rolling. While going through the rail my
door and seat belt were ripped from the car. As we came
out of the ditch and started to roll I was thrown 50' from
the car with only a fractured ankle to show of it. While in
the shock trauma unit I woke up to an internal, in sucked.
I don't remember anything for this was what I was told.
The only thing I do remember is looking at my best friend
and not knowing if he and/or I were dead. Luckily nobody
was dead and we can all talk about it. But lying there I
was told that I was one lucky man, that I should be dead.
My mother told me that almost 16 years to the date I was
in the hospital with the same heart monitor hook ups on
me and was lucky to be alive. I cried. I cried because I was
thankful for being here, but to escape death twice, there is
a reason. A reason I haven't figured out yet but am very
anxious to stumble upon. Your speech has made me think

even harder and gave me another reason to keep on going. I will never give up and you should never either, when tragic things happen you really see all the love others have for you but have just been hiding.

Thank You,
Josh W.

> "Being near death helps us appreciate life. And how sweet life really is."

Letter 36

Hi Mr. Petrocelli,

My name is Gina R. and you have come to my high school before when I was younger a couple years ago. The first time you visited I listened in awe with what you had to say and I understood the message you were spreading—but truthfully I wasn't seeing the big picture. It may be because at that time I hadn't had anything nearly as traumatic happen to me before so I had a hard time associating your true story with real life.

Now I am presently a junior in High School and you came again to give a speech at my school on April 15. Your speech touched me much more than it did the first time; and I know why and am grateful to finally realize first hand what you mean. A few weeks ago on the afternoon of March 24 I was driving home alone from varsity soccer practice. I approached a bad intersection at the top of a hill that I had to make a left turn onto. The road I was turning onto was a highway- you probably know it from living in NY...State Route 9? Well anyway I stopped at the sign and let traffic pass when I didn't see anyone approaching from either direction I proceeded to make my left turn across the highway. The next thing I knew there was a late model Chevy Caprice in my passenger door. Even though the accident did not involve alcohol it still changed how I look at life and how easily it can be taken away. (In truth I am not a member of SADD at my school but no matter because I have always strongly opposed drunk driving and I will never put myself or allow someone else to be in a situation such as that. My older brother has taught me about that and has been through drunk driving accidents.) The other driver hit me at approx. 60 mph and no one knows how I walked away from the accident with minor physical injuries. My car was demolished; after all it was only an '89 Toyota Corolla I had received back in October from my mom. I was wearing my seatbelt and I'm Catholic, my mother always insists that we keep our St. Christopher medals in all our cars and I suppose the combination of the two may have saved my life. My car's driver door had caved in so far that the drivers seat I was in was pushed forwards and tilted toward the windshield, which cracked on impact, the steering wheel was in the radio/console and the dash was all buckled. The trunk somehow also opened when I got hit. I managed to get away with a bruised knee and partially dislocated hip (that I never knew I had till the medics checked me) some glass in my thigh and a bruised breastbone. The other driver was untouched and didn't even need to go to the hospital. I cannot believe how lucky some people like myself are and how unlucky other such as you are. I can not even compare your accident with mine because your was obviously much different, but my car accident helped me realize the whole '10 seconds' idea and made me more personally realize what your speeches are about.

The way you told your story and how you described it so surreal-like almost as you thought it was a dream, I could not understand it the first time I heard you speak.

When I had the car accident I had a similar feeling; I felt as if I was watching myself get hit by another car, it was the strangest thing I've ever felt. I also didn't even know that I was hurt (similar to what you described), I climbed across the passenger seat and never saw any glass or anything wrong with the car I was in. I never knew I was cut or that I hurt my hip or anything until a paramedic told me. I am so glad that I finally got this wake up call as well as another of your speeches which has shown me I am lucky enough to get another chance to the big picture of life and what matters most.

After your speech I was very touched and got your book that I was really happy to have you sign to me and I am currently reading it, among the many other things I try to read as best I can for school. I love how you describe Italian families, my mom grew up in the Bronx and my dad in Brooklyn and Long Island- my mom's cooking is priceless as well: (especially her homemade sweet ravioli!) Mr. Petrocelli, you are a new hero to me now that I have been through a lot in the past month. I have a love for freestyle skiing; my dad started me when I was 3 and up until then Mr. Jean Claude Kelly and Johnny Moseley have been my heroes-I have always wanted to ski like them, but I may have to edit my list now.

I will also like to approach life the way you do and realize that everything happens for a reason and there are ways to get your head around whatever may come your way. And that- as I am sure you also know- are no small feat. I know you probably get many e-mails and letters such as this so I understand perfectly if you do not have the time to respond back to me on this. Whatever the case may be I just want to thank you most sincerely for everything that you stand for and for giving speeches like the one you gave to our school all the time I hopes that you will touch even one person. You certainly touched me.

Thanks again,

Gina R.

Section 10

"Touching one's heart is also touching one's soul."

Subj: **You touched my heart =)**

Bobby,

This is Danielle B.; I am 17 and a junior in High School here in Indiana. You came to talk to us today. I am the girl that came up to you after everyone left, just to shake your hand and tell you that you helped me a lot. Then when I looked up into your eyes I started crying. I started to cry because you were talking me as a person. You looked into MY eyes. I was just not part of the crowd you came to talk to. Do you remember me? You are such a great speaker. I would give anything to hear you again. I just wanted to tell you that you really made me think. I will always remember you and what you said. I look up to you in so many ways. You are such a great inspiration to me. I am going to get all of your books. I hope that next year when you come back to our school I can hear you talk again. I will try everything I can to get out of class to see you. What you said today is all I have been thinking about. I know what you said today would help a lot of people this weekend. Prom is a big deal and I know a lot of people are going to think about you and what you had to go through before they take that drink or open that door to drive home. I KNOW I WILL. I hope we can keep in touch over the computer. I know you have a lot of people to write back to and everything so whenever you get a chance. I will check my mail every day. You told me you would be on at 9 your time, 8 my time, but I doubt I will be home. This is why I am writing you this letter. So thank you so much, and I will always have you in my heart. You and your wife and kids will be in my prayers=)

DANIELLE B., Ft. Wayne, IN

> "Conquering fear is one of the greatest victories you can win."

Letter 38

Dear Bobby,

You came to my school in Wilmington, Delaware last year. I was a sophomore at the time, and since then of course I read your book and it was very moving. I've read it 3 times since then! Anyway...the presentation you gave at Padua was amazing; you made me realize how precious life is. I got your book and when I did, you signed it, and then I started to cry because when I was a freshman at Padua in October my best friend was on her way to my house to come over and she was in her new red Mustang because her birthday was 2 days before and she got hit by a drunk driver and after that I was of course depressed and in tears, we have been best friends since we were two years old. I then felt guilty, if I hadn't asked her to come over then none of this would have happened right? Wrong, I realized a whole year later, it was not my fault, from your presentation I learned it wasn't my fault, you personally told me "it wasn't my fault" and that "I would get through it" "it may take time" you said "but I would get through it" and you know what, you were exactly right! I did get through it and now I can talk about what happened and not be in tears at the end. So thank you for helping me realize it wasn't my fault. And the whole 10 seconds thing is totally true. Because I was recently in a snowmobile accident with my other best friend and within 10 seconds we were hit from behind, my head slammed into the ground, the snowmobile ran over my foot, I was knocked out, then it ran into my friend Amy and she got knocked out from the snowmobile running into the back of her helmet~and in 10 seconds this all happened. So your theory is totally 100% TRUE! So thank you for touching my life and helping me realize a few things and you did help me through something I will never forget!

Now I need to ask you a question…would it be at all possible for you to come and talk to my Church youth group? Because I know there are some teens in there who don't take life seriously at all and that's why they have to go to youth group and I want your story to help them REALIZE how precious life really is because I care for each and every one of them, and I love them all very much! It's located in Wilmington Delaware; it's the St. Mary Magdalene Church Youth Group! Thank you, for taking your time to read this, I appreciate it! And I would also appreciate it, if you could reply to my letter, I will be patient! Thank You, God Bless! Love Always,

Kelsey K.
Wilmington, DE

Section 11

"HOPE IS A GOOD THING, MAYBE EVEN THE BEST OF THINGS—AND GOOD THINGS NEVER DIE."

"No matter how many bad decisions you make, it only takes ONE DECISION to turn your life around."

Final Thoughts

Our greatest desire is that you will come away from reading this book with a renewed sense of Hope. I know that the letters that you've read in this book have been an inspiration to you. They were written by people just like you and I who are making the choice to triumph over any adversity that may come their way. When life throws you a curveball, you can have the power and hope to hit it. I want to challenge you to take one more bold and life altering step. Take action in making the "10 Second Principle" an active and real part of your life. Remember that we all make mistakes. There is nothing you could have ever done, or anything that someone has done to you that can't be turned around for good. After you have begun to practice this simple principle, I promise it will change your life in a positive way! Then share it with someone else who needs to know it. If we all will live our lives by making good choices 10 seconds at a time, we surely will see a change in our families, our schools, our communities and our society.

Meet Bobby Petrocelli

In the recent wake of the United States' most devastating terrorist tragedy, countless numbers of people have experienced heartbreaking sudden unexpected deaths of both friends, and loved ones. Bobby Petrocelli's powerful message of healing and hope will inspire, encourage and empower all that hear or read about him.

One of the top motivational speakers in America, Bobby uses his riveting personal story—of how one decision changed his life forever! By no means is he a victim. A drunk driver, crashing through his bedroom and killing his wife, didn't stop him. Instead, he turned his TRAGEDY into TRIUMPH. ***10 SECONDS CHANGED HIS LIFE FOREVER!***

Educating people on the power of good decision making is of utmost importance to Bobby. As an Author, Educator and Motivational Speaker, he is an excellent communicator. His unforgettable story of how he's been able to overcome an incredible amount of adversity completely captivates audiences of all ages, inspiring them to live lives full of passion, faith, love and forgiveness. Those who hear him speak in person, always leave motivated by his uplifting testimonial and refreshed by his charismatic personality. He travels worldwide where millions have gained an endearing sense of hope through one of Bobby's energetic and powerfully charged programs that he always delivers in his own enthusiastic and humorous way!

After successfully competing in baseball for the #1 Ranked College baseball team in the country, upon graduation he spent 11 years teaching, counseling and coaching. He holds a Masters degree in Counseling and a B. S. in Health and Physical Education.

He has authored and co-authored seven different motivational books including his powerful autobiography, <u>Triumph Over Tragedy</u>. In addition to his compelling story, he has co-authored the <u>Teen Power</u> series, <u>Lead Now</u> and <u>The Making of an Unshakable Character</u>. His story has been aired in over 100 countries and has been featured on "Geraldo", "Sally Jesse Raphael", "The Hour of Power", "God Squad", "The Family Channel", <u>Woman's World Magazine</u>, as well as numerous newspapers, magazines and radio programs. His zest for life and sincere love for people is evident to all that come in contact with him.

Bobby enjoys the great outdoors—hiking in the mountains, swimming, boating and water sports and traveling to new places; but ***his greatest joy is spending time with the three most important people in his life— his beautiful wife Suzanne and their two boys, Alec and Aron.***

Bobby Petrocelli, 10 Seconds, Inc.
P.O. Box 923
Bellport, NY 11713
800-547-7933
www.10seconds.org

www.10secondscanchangeyourlifeforever.com

ORDER EXTRA COPIES OF THIS BOOK OR OTHERS BY BOBBY PETROCELLI!

1-10 - $15.00 each.

All Orders of 10 or more Books Available for Discount- Contact our Office. Shipping & Handling charges included in cost:

Other Books by Bobby Petrocelli:

<u>Triumph Over Tragedy</u>: ***Bobby Petrocelli's Biography***

<u>The Making of Unshakable Character</u>: ***Daily Lessons to Build Your Life On***

<u>Lead Now or Step Aside</u>: ***Handbook for Student Leaders***

<u>Teen Empower</u>: ***Advice for those who Teach, Lead & Guide Today's Youth***

<u>Teen Power & Beyond</u>: ***Solid Gold Advice for Young Adults***

<u>Teen Power- Faith Issues</u>: ***Solid Gold Principles & Timeless Truths***

3 WAYS TO ORDER ANY OF BOBBY PETROCELLI'S BOOKS!

Phone: Call 800-547-7933

Website: www.10seconds.org

Mail:

    Bobby Petrocelli, 10 Seconds, Inc.

    P.O. Box 923

    Bellport, NY 11713

Number of Books: _____

Total Price: _____

    Make checks payable to:

    10 Seconds, Inc.

Name: _____

Organization: _____

Street Address: _____

City: _____ State _____ZIP_____

Phone: (_____)- _____-_____

Fax: _____

E-Mail: _____